Simple Strawberry Sensations!

By Laura York

Co-Produced with Karen Fate

Illustrated by Donna Morrison
Cover by Geraldine Hayes

www.simple-sensations.com
Fundraising available.
813-832-4482

This book is dedicated to several people, my Granny who instilled a true love for cooking (and eating!) good food, my loving parents who have always been there for me, and all of my friends, both close and through television, who encouraged me to pursue my love of cooking.

I also must recognize a woman who has given me a tremendous amount of courage through her television show and magazine...Oprah Winfrey. We have never met but her positive approach to life has greatly influenced me. My business partner, Karen Fate, and I truly had an "ah-ha moment" when we decided to follow our hearts and make this book a reality. We refer to ourselves as "Oprah-ites" and we hope that others will be inspired to follow their dreams.

Simple Strawberry Sensations!

Published by
Simple Sensations Marketing, LLC
533 S. Howard Avenue #855
Tampa, Florida 33606
Copyright 2001

Library of Congress Catalog Number: 2001 126099
ISBN: 0-9707086-0-2

Printed by
Rose Printing Company, Inc.
Tallahassee, Florida

Color Separations by
Dimension, Inc.
Tampa, Florida

Graphic Design by
Bayou Graphics, Inc.
Tampa, Florida

Manufactured in the United States of America
First Printing: 2001   25,000 copies

Table of Contents

Strawberries...they're simply sensational!

My passion for strawberries is a result of living in Tampa, Florida. We are blessed with an early crop of these flavorful jewels just in time for Christmas. I love to surprise my family from Kentucky with a decadent treat for the holidays featuring our fabulous fruit.

Just down the road from Tampa is Plant City, which is known as the "Winter Strawberry Capital" of the world. Boy, oh boy, do they know how to celebrate their incredible bounty! Since 1930, The Florida Strawberry Festival has heralded their outstanding crop and ranks as one of the nation's finest annual events. The festival features everything from the hottest music stars, to an unbelievable midway, racing pigs (my personal favorite!) and of course, tons of sweet, red strawberries.

My goal with **Simple Strawberry Sensations** is to further our passion for this fantastic fruit. The challenge was to push the envelope a little and marry some other flavors with the luscious fruit. My hope is that you'll find these recipes interesting and delicious.

Chocolate, both dark and white have always been some of my personal favorites. The combination is a real show-stopper and gave birth to *Strawberry White Chocolate Tiramisu, Dark & White Chocolate Strawberry Pie* and *Unbelievable Chocolate Strawberry Shortcakes.*

Strawberries are also a perfect way to start your day, which led to the many brunch recipes. Be sure to try *Tasty Strawberry-Stuffed French Toast with Warm Strawberry Syrup, Strawberry Macadamia Nut Scones* and *Incredible Strawberry Streusel Muffins*...your family and guests will sing your praises.

My love of vegetables made creating the strawberry salads a snap. I've included my *Super Special Strawberry Salad* which was the Grand Champion Winner at the 1989 Florida Strawberry Festival. New favorites are *Strawberry & Avocado Salad with Orange Dressing, Strawberry & Smoked Turkey Luncheon Salad* and *Spirited Strawberries & Pineapple with Ginger.*

You'll find several delicious beverages, like *Zippy Strawberry Iced Tea, Strawberry Pucker Punch* and *Splashy Strawberry Mimosas.* They're great for parties and family gatherings.

And finally, there are some snappy gift ideas. *Spicy & Sweet Bar-b-que Sauce* is a fantastic new twist. In fact, when I tested it on several of my friends, we literally ran out of grilled chicken while trying to enjoy every drop of the sauce! It's incredible.

I want to thank Karen Fate, Elizabeth Spitler and Alysia Ekizian for helping me test these recipes. Also, a big thanks to all of my friends for putting their diets on hold and picking up their forks to try these recipes.

Most of these recipes are very simple and straightforward. A few recipes do require a little extra time and effort, like *Sassy Strawberry Tacos* and *Surprisingly Simple Tuxedo Strawberries* but they're worth it. I hope you'll enjoy them!

Laura York

Showy Strawberries for Brunch

Tasty Strawberry-Stuffed French Toast

1 (8-ounce) package cream cheese,
  softened
1/2 cup powdered sugar
1 Tablespoon vanilla extract
1/2 teaspoon cinnamon
8 slices bread, white or whole wheat
3 cups strawberries, hulled and sliced
3 eggs, beaten
2 Tablespoons milk
4 Tablespoons butter (optional)
2 Tablespoons powdered sugar, sifted

In a small bowl, combine the cream cheese, 1/2 cup powdered sugar, vanilla extract and cinnamon; mix until smooth. Spread one side of each slice of bread evenly with the cream cheese mixture. On the cream cheese side of four slices of the bread, layer with some sliced strawberries evenly over the surface of each slice. Top each slice with a remaining slice of bread, pressing the cream cheese side down onto the strawberries. Press together gently to seal strawberries inside sandwich.

In a shallow bowl, combine the eggs and milk; mix well and set aside.

Preheat oven to 200° F. Spray a large baking sheet lightly with cooking spray and place in oven. Spray a large nonstick skillet with cooking spray or melt 1 Tablespoon butter in skillet over medium-high heat.

Dip strawberry sandwiches into the egg mixture, turning to soak each side. Place soaked sandwich in the hot skillet and cook on each side until browned. Remove sandwich from skillet and place on baking sheet in warm oven and repeat until all sandwiches are cooked.

Just before serving, cut each sandwich diagonally; top with remaining strawberries and sprinkle with 2 Tablespoons powdered sugar. Serve with *Warm Strawberry Syrup* (page 7).

Yield: 4 servings

Warm Strawberry Syrup

1/2 cup maple syrup
2 Tablespoons orange juice or
   Grand Marnier
3/4 cup puréed strawberries

In a small saucepan, combine the maple syrup, orange juice and puréed strawberries.
Heat mixture over medium heat for 5 minutes or until thickened slightly, stirring
frequently. Serve while warm.

Yield: approximately 1 1/2 cups

Strawberry Buttermilk Pancakes

2 cups flour
2 Tablespoons sugar
2 teaspoons baking powder
1 teaspoon baking soda
1/2 teaspoon salt
1 1/2 teaspoons cinnamon
2 cups buttermilk
2 eggs, beaten
2 Tablespoons butter, melted
1/2 cup strawberries, hulled and sliced
Vegetable oil or butter

In a medium bowl, combine flour, sugar, baking powder, baking soda, salt and cinnamon; mix well. Add buttermilk, eggs and butter, stirring just until combined. Gently fold sliced strawberries into batter.

Preheat oven to 200° F. Spray a large baking sheet lightly with cooking spray and place in oven.

Heat a large skillet, adding a little vegetable oil or butter to coat the pan. Ladle a 5-inch circle of batter into the skillet; cook pancakes until the tops are covered with tiny bubbles, then flip them over and finish cooking. Place pancakes on baking sheet in warm oven. Repeat process until all batter is used.

Serve with *Warm Strawberry Syrup* (page 7).

Yield: 12 pancakes

Strawberry Brunch Waffles

1 (18-ounce) package yellow cake mix
1 1/2 cups half-and-half
4 eggs, beaten
1/2 teaspoon salt
1/2 teaspoon almond extract
4 cups strawberries, hulled and sliced
1/4 cup sugar
1/4 cup powdered sugar

In a medium bowl, combine cake mix, half-and-half, eggs, salt and almond extract; mix until smooth and set aside.

In a medium bowl, combine strawberries and sugar; mix well and set aside.

Spray a waffle iron with cooking spray and heat to medium-high heat.

Pour about 1 cup of batter into waffle iron for a 9-inch waffle. Bake until golden brown. Place waffle on a wire rack to cool. Continue baking waffles until all batter is used.

Sprinkle waffles with powdered sugar. Top with sweetened strawberries and serve. *Warm Strawberry Syrup* (page 7) may be served on the side.

Yield: 6 to 8 servings

Strawberry French Toast Bake

French Toast:
1 (8-ounce) loaf crusty
   French bread
2 1/4 cups milk
4 eggs, beaten
3 Tablespoons sugar
1/2 teaspoon salt
1 teaspoon cinnamon
1 Tablespoon vanilla extract
2 cups strawberries,
   hulled and sliced

Topping:
1/2 cup flour
1/2 cup light brown sugar,
   packed
1/2 cup pecans, chopped
1/3 cup butter

For the French Toast: Slice 1/2-inch off each end of French bread loaf, then cut into 10 slices.

Spray a 9 x 13-inch baking dish with cooking spray. Arrange the bread slices in a single layer in the baking dish.

In a medium bowl, combine the milk, eggs, sugar, salt, cinnamon and vanilla extract; mix until sugar is dissolved. Pour mixture over bread. Chill, covered, for 6 hours or overnight.

Sprinkle 1 cup of the sliced strawberries over soaked bread.

Preheat the oven to 375° F.

For the Topping: In a small bowl, combine the flour, brown sugar and pecans; mix well. Using a pastry blender, cut in the butter until crumbly. Sprinkle the topping over the soaked bread and strawberries.

Bake for 35 to 40 minutes or until set and golden brown. Remove from oven and sprinkle with remaining strawberries.

Warm Strawberry Syrup (page 7) may be served on the side.

Yield: 4 to 6 servings

Strawberry Macadamia Nut Scones

2 1/2 cups flour
1/3 cup light brown sugar, packed
2 1/2 teaspoons baking powder
1/4 teaspoon salt
1/3 cup butter, chilled, cut into pieces
1 cup strawberries,
   coarsely chopped
2 eggs
1 teaspoon vanilla extract
3/4 cup macadamia nuts, toasted,
   lightly salted and chopped
1 Tablespoon sugar
1/4 teaspoon cinnamon

Preheat oven to 375° F. Lightly spray a baking sheet with cooking spray; set aside.

In a large bowl, combine flour, brown sugar, baking powder and salt; mix well. Using a pastry blender, cut in the butter until it resembles coarse crumbs.

In a small bowl, combine strawberries, eggs and vanilla extract; mix well. Add strawberry mixture to the flour mixture and stir to combine. The dough will be sticky. Stir in nuts.

Spread the dough into a 9-inch circle in the center of the prepared pan.

In a small bowl, combine sugar and cinnamon; sprinkle over dough. Using a serrated knife, cut the dough into 8 wedges.

Bake for 30 to 35 minutes or until golden brown and a cake tester or wooden pick inserted into the center of the scones comes out clean.

Cool in the pan on a wire rack for 5 minutes then remove from pan and place on wire rack to cool completely.

Serve warm, room temperature, or split horizontally and toast. *Strawberry Orange Butter Spread* (page 74) is great with these scones.

Yield: 8 servings

Baked Strawberries & Fruit Casserole

2 cups strawberries, hulled and halved
1 (16-ounce) can sliced pears, drained,
2 (16-ounce) cans sliced peaches,
   drained
1 (16-ounce) can apricot halves, drained
1 (16-ounce) can pineapple chunks,
   drained
1 cup light brown sugar, packed
1/2 cup butter, melted
2 teaspoons curry powder
1/2 teaspoon salt

Preheat oven to 325° F.

Spray a large 3-quart casserole dish evenly with cooking spray. Arrange fruits in casserole; set aside.

In a small bowl, combine brown sugar, butter, curry powder and salt; mix well. Pour over fruits.

Bake, uncovered for 1 hour. Serve while hot.

Yield: 10 to 12 servings

Dazzling Strawberry Pizza

Crust:
1 (18-ounce) roll refrigerator
sugar cookies

Creamy Orange Filling:
1 (8-ounce) package cream
cheese, softened
1/2 cup powdered sugar
2 teaspoons orange juice or
Grand Marnier

Fruit Topping:
3 cups strawberries, hulled and
sliced
1 (11-ounce) can mandarin
orange slices, drained
2 kiwi, peeled and sliced

Orange Sauce:
1/4 cup orange marmalade
1 teaspoon orange juice or Grand Marnier

For the Crust: Preheat oven to 350° F.

Slice cookie dough into 1/8-inch slices. Layer slices evenly and overlap slightly, pressing lightly onto a 12-inch round pizza pan.

Bake for 10 to 12 minutes or until golden brown. Remove from oven and cool completely on a wire rack.

For the Orange Filling: In a small bowl, combine the filling ingredients and mix until smooth. Spread evenly over cooled crust.

For the Fruit Topping: Arrange fruits on top of filling. You may form rings with the fruit for a pretty presentation.

For the Orange Sauce: In a small saucepan, combine orange marmalade and orange juice. Melt over low heat, stirring constantly. Remove from heat and cool for 2 minutes. Spoon sauce over fruits.

Chill, covered, until ready to serve. Cut into wedges.

Yield: 12 servings

Incredible Strawberry Streusel Muffins

Muffins:
2 cups flour
1/3 cup sugar
1/3 cup light brown sugar, packed
2 teaspoons baking powder
1/2 teaspoon salt
1 teaspoon cinnamon
1/2 teaspoon nutmeg
1 egg, beaten
1/2 cup butter, melted
1/2 cup half-and-half
1 1/2 cups strawberries, hulled and sliced
1 Tablespoon orange zest

Streusel Topping:
3/4 cup pecans, chopped
1/2 cup light brown sugar, packed
1/4 cup flour
2 teaspoons cinnamon
1/4 teaspoon nutmeg
2 teaspoons orange zest
2 Tablespoons butter, melted

Orange Glaze:
3/4 cup powdered sugar
1 Tablespoon plus 1 teaspoon orange
   juice

For the Muffins: Preheat oven to 350° F.

In a medium bowl, sift together the flour, sugar, brown sugar, baking powder, salt, cinnamon and nutmeg; set aside.

In a small bowl, combine the egg, butter and half-and-half; mix well. Pour the egg mixture into the flour mixture and stir just until moistened. Fold in the strawberries and orange zest. Spoon into 12 greased muffin cups.

For the Streusel Topping: In a small bowl, combine the pecans, brown sugar, flour, cinnamon, nutmeg and orange zest; mix well. Stir in the butter and mix well. Sprinkle evenly over the muffins.

Bake for 20 to 25 minutes or until golden brown. Remove from oven and cool completely on a wire rack.

For the Orange Glaze: In a small bowl, combine the powdered sugar and orange juice; mix well. Drizzle glaze over cooled muffins.

Yield: 1 dozen

So Simple Strawberry Melon Bowls

2 medium cantaloupes
2 cups strawberries, hulled and halved
$1/3$ cup orange juice
$1/3$ cup orange marmalade
1 teaspoon lemon juice
$1/2$ cup pecans, chopped

Cut cantaloupes in half and remove the seeds. Using a melon-ball scoop, scoop out melon balls and place in a medium bowl; set aside. On the bottom of each melon shell, cut off a $1/2$-inch slice to allow the melon shell to sit flat on a baking sheet. Chill, covered, until ready to use.

Add the strawberries to the cantaloupe balls and set aside.

In a small bowl, combine the orange juice, orange marmalade and lemon juice; mix well. Pour the orange juice mixture over the fruit and toss gently. Chill, covered, until ready to use.

To serve, spoon fruit into cantaloupe shells and sprinkle with the pecans.

Yield: 4 servings

Strawberry Ambrosia Kabobs

1 pint strawberries, hulled
1 fresh pineapple, peeled, cored and
    cubed
2 cups white seedless grapes
16 large marshmallows
1 cup sweetened coconut flakes
1/4 cup orange juice
1/4 cup orange marmalade
8 to 10 bamboo skewers

In a large bowl, combine strawberries, pineapple, grapes, marshmallows and coconut; toss to mix.

In a small bowl, combine orange juice and orange marmalade; mix well. Pour orange juice mixture over fruit and toss lightly to combine. Chill, covered, for 4 hours or overnight.

Up to 2 hours before serving, thread fruits and marshmallows on bamboo skewers and place on a serving platter. Chill, covered, until ready to serve.

Yield: 8 to 10 servings

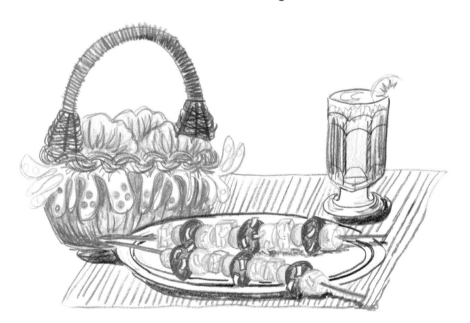

Delicious Strawberry Bread

3 cups flour
1 teaspoon baking soda
1/2 teaspoon salt
1 Tablespoon cinnamon
2 cups sugar
4 eggs, beaten
2 cups strawberries, hulled and sliced
1 1/2 cups vegetable oil
1 1/2 cups pecans, coarsely chopped

Preheat oven to 325° F. Generously grease two 5 x 9-inch loaf pans; set aside.

In a medium bowl, sift together the flour, baking soda, salt, cinnamon and sugar; set aside.

In another medium bowl, combine eggs, strawberries and oil; mix well. Gradually add the flour mixture, stirring to combine completely. Add the pecans and mix well. Pour the batter equally into the two prepared loaf pans.

Bake for 1 hour or until a wooden pick inserted into the center of the loaf comes out clean.

Cool bread in pans on a wire rack for 5 minutes, then turn bread out onto racks to cool completely.

Yield: 2 loaves

Splashy Strawberry Beverages

Pride of Kentucky Strawberry Julep

1 cup puréed strawberries
1 Tablespoon sugar
4 cups shaved ice
1 cup bourbon
4 mint sprigs
4 strawberries, whole with caps

In a small bowl, combine the
puréed strawberries and sugar;
mix until the sugar is dissolved.
Divide the strawberry mixture
equally among four tall glasses.
Pack each glass with 1 cup of shaved ice. Pour 1/4 cup bourbon
into each glass. Garnish each with a mint sprig and a whole strawberry.

Yield: 4 servings

Splashy Strawberry Mimosas

3 cups fresh orange juice, chilled
1 pint strawberries, hulled and halved
2 Tablespoons sugar
1 bottle dry champagne, chilled
6 to 8 strawberries, whole with caps

In a blender, combine orange juice, strawberry halves and sugar; blend until smooth.
Pour mixture into a large pitcher. Add the champagne and stir. Pour into tall champagne
glasses. Take whole strawberries and cut a slit halfway from the bottom of each berry
toward the cap. Place a prepared strawberry on the lip of each glass.

Yield: 6 to 8 servings

Go Ape Strawberry Shake!

1 1/2 cups strawberries, hulled and
   halved
1 ripe banana, sliced
1 (14-ounce) can sweetened condensed
   milk
1 cup ice water
1/3 cup orange juice, chilled
2 to 3 cups ice

In a blender, combine strawberries, banana, condensed milk, ice water and orange juice; blend until smooth. Gradually add ice and continue blending until smooth. Serve in tall glasses.

Yield: 4 servings

Sunny Strawberry Orange Smoothie

1/2 cup strawberries, hulled and halved
1/2 cup pineapple chunks
1/2 cup orange juice

In a blender, combine strawberries, pineapple and orange juice; blend until smooth. Serve immediately.

You may try freezing fruits before blending or add 4 ice cubes while blending for a frosty smoothie.

Yield: 1 serving

Sparkling Strawberry Champagne Punch

2 quarts strawberries, hulled and halved
1/2 cup powdered sugar
2 liters champagne, chilled, chilled
2 (1-liter) bottles club soda, chilled

In a blender or food processor, combine the strawberries and powdered sugar; blend until smooth. Pour the mixture through a fine sieve into a medium bowl; discard seeds and pulp. Chill, covered, until ready to use.

Just before serving, pour the strawberry juice into a large punch bowl. Add the champagne and club soda; stir to mix.

Fill a decorative dish, larger than the punch bowl, with ice. Set the punch bowl in the ice-filled dish to keep the punch cold without diluting it.

Yield: 20 to 24 servings

Strawberry Pucker Punch

2 cups strawberries, hulled and halved
1 (12-ounce) can frozen lemonade
   concentrate, thawed
1 (2-liter) bottle ginger ale, chilled
1 pint lemon-lime sherbet

In a blender or food processor, purée strawberries.

In a large punch bowl, combine strawberry purée, lemonade concentrate and ginger ale; mix well. Spoon the sherbet into the punch and stir to dissolve.

Float a *Crystal Strawberry Ice Ring* (below) in the punch bowl to keep the punch cold.

Yield: 16 to 18 servings

Crystal Strawberry Ice Ring

Distilled water
Strawberries, whole with caps

Fill a ring mold or plastic bowl with a $1/2$ inch distilled water and freeze. Place strawberries on top of the ice layer and fill with enough distilled water to just cover the strawberries; freeze. Add additional water to a $1/2$ inch below top of mold and freeze.

To unmold, turn mold upside down and run warm water over mold to loosen ice ring. Wrap ice ring in plastic wrap and place on a baking sheet then store ice ring in freezer until ready to use.

Float ice ring, fruit side up, in a punch bowl.

The distilled water will remain crystal clear when frozen.

Yield: 1 ice ring

Zippy Strawberry Iced Tea

2 cups strawberries, hulled and halved
1/2 cup sugar
6 cups water
2 tea bags, single serving size
1 (12-ounce) can frozen lemonade
   concentrate, thawed
1 (1-liter) bottle club soda, chilled
Ice

In a blender or food processor, purée strawberries.

In a small bowl, combine the strawberry purée and sugar; mix until sugar is dissolved. Chill, covered, until ready to use.

In a medium saucepan, heat the water to a rapid boil; remove from the heat and steep the tea bags for 5 minutes. Remove tea bags and cool the tea to room temperature.

In a large pitcher or punch bowl, combine the strawberry purée and lemonade concentrate; mix well. Add the cooled tea and club soda; mix well.

Serve over ice.

Yield: 12 servings

Splendid Strawberry
Soups
&
Salads

Chilled Strawberry Soup

5 cups strawberries, hulled and halved
1/2 cup sugar
2 cups orange juice
2 cups vanilla yogurt
10 strawberries, hulled and sliced
   lengthwise in 4 slices
2 teaspoons orange zest

In a blender or food processor, purée 5 cups strawberries.

In a large pitcher, combine strawberry purée, sugar, orange juice and yogurt; mix well. Chill, covered, for 6 hours.

To serve, ladle soup into serving bowls. Carefully lay 5 strawberry slices in the center of each serving to form a strawberry star floating on top of the soup. Sprinkle each with 1/4 teaspoon orange zest.

Yield: 8 servings

Spunky Strawberry Sangria Soup

3 cups strawberries, hulled and halved
1 1/2 cups orange juice
1 cup sangria
1/2 cup sugar
2 Tablespoons lemon juice
1/4 teaspoon cinnamon
1 cup whipping cream
1/2 cup sour cream

In a blender or food processor, purée strawberries; set aside.

In a large saucepan, combine orange juice, sangria, sugar, lemon juice and cinnamon; mix well. Place pan over medium-high heat and bring to a boil. Reduce heat to medium and simmer for 10 minutes, stirring frequently. Add strawberry purée and return to a boil. Reduce heat and cook for an additional 10 minutes, stirring frequently. Remove from heat and cool.

In a medium bowl, whip cream until stiff peaks form. Fold in sour cream. Fold cooled strawberry mixture into whipped cream mixture.

Serve at room temperature or chilled.

Yield: 1 1/2 quarts

Strawberry & Avocado Salad with Orange Dressing

Orange Dressing:
1/3 cup vegetable oil
3 Tablespoons red wine vinegar
3 Tablespoons orange juice
6 drops red pepper sauce
1/4 teaspoon salt
Dash of black pepper

Salad:
1 pint strawberries, hulled and sliced
3 kiwi, peeled and sliced
1 head Boston Bibb lettuce or Romaine
  lettuce, torn into bite-size pieces
1 avocado, peeled, seeded and cut into
  bite-size pieces
2 teaspoons lemon juice

For the Orange Dressing: In a small bowl, whisk together the Orange Dressing ingredients until blended. Chill, covered, until ready to use.

For the Salad: In a large salad bowl, combine strawberries, kiwi and lettuce; toss to mix. Chill, covered, until ready to use.

In a small bowl, toss avocado and lemon juice. Chill, covered, until ready to use.

Just before serving, add avocado to salad and toss with the Orange Dressing.

Yield: 6 servings

Super Special Strawberry Salad

Grand Champion Winner, the 1989 Florida Strawberry Festival, Plant City, FL

Glazed Almond Topping:
1/4 cup sliced almonds
1 Tablespoon plus 1 teaspoon sugar

Salad:
1 large bunch romaine lettuce,
   torn into bite-size pieces
2 stalks of celery, chopped
2 1/2 cups strawberries, hulled and sliced
1 (11-ounce) can mandarin oranges,
   drained

Sweet & Sour Dressing:
1/4 cup vegetable oil
2 Tablespoons sugar
2 Tablespoons vinegar
1/2 teaspoon salt
6 drops red pepper sauce
Dash of black pepper

For the Glazed Almond Topping: In a small skillet, cook almonds and sugar over low heat, stirring constantly until sugar is melted and almonds are coated. Sprinkle almonds onto a sheet of waxed paper; let cool. Break the almonds apart and set aside.

For the Salad: In a large salad bowl, toss the salad ingredients until combined.

For the Sweet & Sour Dressing: In a small container with a tight lid, combine the Sweet & Sour Dressing ingredients and shake to combine.

Pour the dressing over salad and toss to combine. Sprinkle the Glazed Almond Topping over the salad and serve immediately.

Yield: 4 to 6 servings

Crispy & Creamy Strawberry Salad

Strawberry Dressing:

1 1/2 cups strawberries, hulled and halved
2 Tablespoons red wine vinegar
2 Tablespoons light brown sugar, packed
1/4 cup olive oil
6 drops red pepper sauce
1 teaspoon lemon juice
1/2 teaspoon salt
Dash of black pepper

Salad:

6 cups Romaine lettuce,
   torn into bite-size pieces
2 cups strawberries, hulled
   and halved
1 (8-ounce) can sliced water chestnuts,
   drained
1/2 cup pistachios, chopped

For the Strawberry Dressing: In a food processor or blender, place the Strawberry Dressing ingredients and blend until smooth. Chill, covered, until ready to use.

For the Salad: In a large salad bowl, combine lettuce, strawberries and water chestnuts; toss to combine.

Just before serving, pour Strawberry Dressing over salad and toss to combine. Sprinkle salad with pistachios.

You may add 2 to 2 1/2 cups chopped cooked chicken to make a great main course salad.

Yield: 8 servings

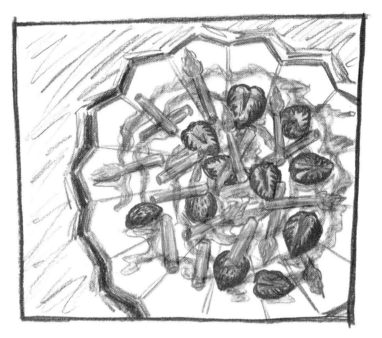

Strawberries & Asparagus with Strawberry Vinaigrette

2¹/2 pounds fresh asparagus
¹/4 cup red wine vinegar
¹/2 cup extra-virgin olive oil
2 teaspoons honey
2 cups strawberries, hulled and halved

Trim asparagus and steam it until tender-crisp. Plunge asparagus immediately into ice water and cool completely. Drain and cut each stalk into thirds.

In a small bowl, combine the vinegar, olive oil and honey; mix well.

In a medium bowl, combine the asparagus and strawberries; toss to mix. Pour the Strawberry Vinaigrette over the mixture and toss gently. Chill, covered, for 1 hour before serving.

Yield: 6 servings

Strawberry & Smoked Turkey Luncheon Salad

Salad:
1 large fresh pineapple
3 cups smoked turkey breasts, chopped
1 cup strawberries, hulled and halved
1/2 cup whole almonds, blanched
2 kiwi, peeled and sliced

Dressing:
1 (3-ounce) package cream cheese,
   softened
1 Tablespoon sugar
4 Tablespoons orange juice
6 drops red pepper sauce

Garnish:
2 bunches green onion tops

For the Salad: Lay the pineapple on its side and cut three 3/4-inch slices crosswise from the center of the pineapple. Cut each slice into six even wedges and remove the core; set wedges aside in refrigerator. Peel, core and coarsely chop the remaining pineapple.

In a medium bowl, combine the chopped pineapple, turkey, strawberries, almonds and kiwi.

For the Dressing: In a small bowl, mix the cream cheese and sugar until smooth. Add the orange juice and red pepper sauce; mix well.

Pour the dressing over the salad and toss gently to combine. Chill, covered, until ready to serve.

To assemble: Use six individual serving plates. Toward the bottom of each plate, arrange three of the pineapple wedges with the tips touching to form a starburst design. Fan a few green onion tops out and place on plate to form the top of pineapple design. Spoon the salad in the center of the pineapple starburst. Chill, covered until ready to serve.

Yield: 6 servings

Strawberry & Spinach Salad with Poppy Seed Dressing

Poppy Seed Dressing:

1/4 cup apple cider vinegar
1/4 cup red wine vinegar
1/2 cup vegetable oil
1/3 cup sugar
1 Tablespoon poppy seeds
1/4 teaspoon paprika

Salad:

2 Tablespoons butter
3/4 cup slivered almonds
1 pound spinach, torn into
   bite-size pieces
1 pint strawberries, hulled
   and sliced
1/2 cup green onions, chopped

For the Poppy Seed Dressing: In a small mixing bowl, combine the Poppy Seed Dressing ingredients and mix well. Chill, covered, until ready to use.

For the Salad: In a small skillet, melt the butter over medium-high heat and sauté almonds until golden brown. Remove from heat and transfer to a plate to cool.

In a large salad bowl, toss together spinach, strawberries, green onions and almonds.

Just before serving, pour Poppy Seed Dressing over salad and toss to combine.

Yield: 6 to 8 servings

Quick Strawberry & Feta Cheese Salad

Dressing:
1/2 cup sugar
1/2 cup red wine vinegar
1/2 teaspoon dry mustard
1/2 cup vegetable oil
1/2 teaspoon salt
1/2 teaspoon red pepper sauce
1 Tablespoon garlic, minced

Salad:
3 heads Boston Bibb lettuce, torn into
   bite-size pieces
1 pint strawberries, hulled and sliced
1/2 pound feta cheese, crumbled

For the Dressing: In a small saucepan, combine sugar and vinegar; mix well. Place over medium-high heat and stir until sugar is dissolved. Remove from heat and stir in mustard, oil, salt, red pepper sauce and garlic; mix well. Chill, covered, until ready to use.

For the Salad: On a large serving platter, arrange the lettuce to form an even layer. Arrange the strawberries over the lettuce. Sprinkle with the feta cheese.

Just before serving, drizzle the dressing over the salad.

Yield: 6 to 8 servings

Asian Strawberry Pasta Salad

Salad:

2 cups strawberries, hulled and halved
2 cups bok choy (Chinese Cabbage), shredded
1 cup bean sprouts
1 (8-ounce) can sliced water chestnuts, drained
8 ounces angel hair pasta, or thin spaghetti, cooked according to package directions and drained
1/4 cup cilantro, chopped

Dressing:

2 Tablespoons vegetable oil
2 Tablespoons chicken bouillon granules
2 Tablespoons creamy peanut butter
1 teaspoon soy sauce
2 teaspoons honey
1 Tablespoon garlic, minced
1/4 teaspoon ground ginger
1 Tablespoon lemon juice
1/4 teaspoon red pepper sauce
1/2 cup puréed strawberries

Garnish:

1/2 cup roasted peanuts, chopped

For the Salad: In a large salad bowl, combine the salad ingredients and toss gently to mix.

For the Dressing: In a small saucepan, combine the oil, chicken bouillon, peanut butter, soy sauce, honey, garlic, ginger, lemon juice and red pepper sauce; mix well. Simmer over medium-high heat until thickened and smooth, stirring frequently. Remove from heat and stir in the puréed strawberries. Pour the dressing into a bowl and let stand for 10 minutes.

To assemble: Pour the dressing over the salad and garnish with the peanuts. Serve immediately.

Yield: 4 servings

Zesty Strawberry Chicken Curry Salad

I cup mayonnaise
3 Tablespoons fruit chutney or
   spicy chutney
I Tablespoon lemon juice
1/2 teaspoon salt
1/2 teaspoon curry powder
3 cups cooked chicken, chopped
I cup English walnuts, coarsely chopped
I cup celery, chopped
1/2 cup seedless red or green grapes,
   halved
I pint strawberries, hulled and sliced
I head Romaine lettuce, torn into
   bite-size pieces
6 strawberries, whole with caps

In a large bowl, combine the mayonnaise, chutney, lemon juice, salt and curry powder; mix well. Add the chicken, walnuts, celery and grapes; mix well. Chill, covered, for 1 hour.

Just before serving, add sliced strawberries and toss gently to combine.

Spread lettuce on six individual serving plates and spoon chicken salad in the center of each plate. Garnish each plate with a whole strawberry.

Yield: 6 servings

Spirited Strawberries & Pineapple with Ginger

2 (16-ounce) cans pineapple chunks, in
   natural juice
$1/2$ cup sugar
2 Tablespoons lemon juice
2 Tablespoons fresh ginger, grated or
   $1 1/2$ teaspoons ground ginger
2 pints strawberries, hulled and sliced

Drain the pineapple, reserving the juice. Combine the reserved juice with enough water to equal 2 cups.

In a small saucepan, combine the pineapple juice mixture, sugar and lemon juice. Place pan over medium-high heat and bring to a boil, stirring frequently. Add the ginger and simmer for 5 minutes.

In a medium bowl, place pineapple chunks. Pour the hot syrup over the pineapple. Chill, covered, for 6 hours or overnight.

Just before serving, add the strawberries to the pineapple and toss gently to combine.

Yield: 8 servings

Cool Strawberry & Pretzel Salad

Crust:
1/2 cup butter
1 cup pretzels, crushed
3 Tablespoons sugar

Strawberry Layer:
2/3 cup boiling water
1 (6-ounce) package strawberry-flavored
   gelatin
1 1/2 cups orange juice, chilled
1 1/2 cups strawberries, hulled and sliced

Cool & Creamy Layer:
1 cup sugar
1 (8-ounce) package cream cheese,
   softened
1 (8-ounce) container frozen whipped
   topping, thawed

For the Crust: Preheat oven to 350° F. Lightly spray a 9 x 13-inch baking dish with cooking spray.

In a medium saucepan, melt the butter over medium-high heat. Remove from heat and stir in crushed pretzels and sugar; mix well. Press mixture evenly over the bottom of the prepared baking dish.

Bake for 10 minutes. Cool completely on a wire rack.

For the Strawberry Layer: In a medium bowl, pour in the boiling water. Sprinkle the strawberry gelatin into the water and stir until the gelatin is completely dissolved. Stir in the chilled orange juice and strawberries. Chill, covered, until partially set.

For the Cool & Creamy Layer: In a large bowl, combine the sugar and cream cheese; stir until blended. Fold in the whipped topping.

To assemble: Spoon the Cool & Creamy Layer evenly over the pretzel crust. Spread the Strawberry Layer evenly over the Cool & Creamy Layer. Chill, covered, for 2 hours or until set.

Cut into squares and serve.

Yield: 12 servings

Sweet & Salty Strawberry Salad

3 Tablespoons sugar
1/4 cup balsamic vinegar
1/4 teaspoon salt
1/2 teaspoon red pepper sauce
3 cups strawberries, hulled and halved
1/4 cup sunflower seed kernels, salted

In a medium glass bowl, combine sugar, vinegar, salt and red pepper sauce; mix until sugar is dissolved. Add strawberries and toss to coat. Allow the strawberries to marinate for 10 minutes.

Just before serving, toss the strawberries gently and spoon into individual bowls. Sprinkle with sunflower kernels and serve immediately.

Yield: 6 servings

Luscious Strawberries & Fruit Bowl with Peach Sauce

1 (29-ounce) can sliced
   peaches in heavy syrup
1 egg, beaten
3 Tablespoons flour
1 Tablespoon butter
1 Tablespoon lemon juice
1 cup whipping cream
1/4 cup powdered sugar
1/4 teaspoon almond extract
1 (16-ounce) can pineapple
   chunks, in natural juice,
   drained
2 bananas, sliced
2 pints strawberries, hulled and sliced
1 (11-ounce) can mandarin oranges, drained
2 kiwi, peeled and sliced
5 strawberries, whole with caps
1/2 cup slivered almonds, toasted

Drain the peaches, reserving the syrup. In a measuring bowl, combine the reserved syrup with enough water to equal 1 cup.

In a medium saucepan, combine the syrup mixture, egg and flour; mix well. Cook over medium-high heat until thickened. Remove from heat. Stir in the butter and lemon juice; mix well. Cool completely.

In a medium mixing bowl, whip the cream and the powdered sugar until stiff peaks form. Fold the whipped cream into the cooled peach sauce. Chill, covered, until ready to use.

Using a clear glass salad bowl, layer the peaches, pineapple, bananas, sliced strawberries and mandarin oranges. Spread the cooled peach sauce over fruit. Chill, covered, for 6 hours or overnight.

Just before serving, garnish the salad with kiwi slices and whole strawberries. Sprinkle with the toasted almonds.

Yield: 8 to 10 servings

Florida Strawberry & Citrus Salad

3 cups strawberries, hulled and halved,
   divided
1/2 cup orange juice
1/2 cup sugar
1 Tablespoon Grand Marnier
4 seedless oranges, peeled and cut
   crosswise
2 pink grapefruit, peeled and cut
   crosswise
1/2 cup slivered almonds, blanched

In a blender or food processor, purée 3/4 cup strawberries; set aside.

In a medium saucepan, combine the orange juice and sugar. Cook over medium-high heat, stirring until the sugar is dissolved. Add the puréed strawberries and Grand Marnier and cook for 5 minutes, stirring occasionally. Pour the syrup into a small bowl and cool completely.

On a large serving platter or on 6 individual plates, arrange remaining strawberries, oranges and grapefruit. Drizzle the strawberry syrup evenly over the fruits. Chill, covered, for 1 hour.

Just before serving, sprinkle with the almonds.

Yield: 6 servings

Spectacular Strawberry Desserts

Nutty Strawberry Cookies

2^1/$_2$ cups flour
2 teaspoons baking soda
1 teaspoon cinnamon
^{1}/$_4$ teaspoon nutmeg
^{1}/$_4$ teaspoon salt
^{3}/$_4$ cup shortening
2 (3-ounce) packages strawberry-
    flavored gelatin
^{2}/$_3$ cup sugar, divided
1 egg, beaten
^{1}/$_4$ cup light corn syrup
^{1}/$_3$ cup puréed strawberries
^{3}/$_4$ cup pecans, chopped

In a small bowl, sift together the flour, baking soda, cinnamon, nutmeg and salt; set aside.

In a large bowl, combine shortening, gelatin, ^{1}/$_3$ cup sugar and egg; beat until creamy. Add corn syrup, puréed strawberries and pecans; mix well. Blend in flour mixture. Chill, covered, for 1 hour.

Preheat oven to 350° F.

Place ^{1}/$_3$ cup sugar in a small bowl. Shape dough by heaping teaspoonfuls into balls and roll in the sugar to coat completely. Arrange 2 inches apart on an ungreased cookie sheet.

Bake for 15 minutes. Place on cookie sheet on a wire rack for 2 minutes. Remove cookies to wire rack to cool completely.

Yield: 3 dozen cookies

Surprisingly Simple Tuxedo Strawberries

1 (12-ounce) package white chocolate
  chips
1 (12-ounce) package semi-sweet
  chocolate chips
24 strawberries, whole with caps,
  washed and thoroughly dried

Line a baking sheet with a piece of
waxed paper and set aside.

In a 1-cup glass measuring cup, or
other small and tall microwaveable
dish, place half the white chocolate
chips. Microwave on MEDIUM-HIGH (70%) for 1 minute; stir. Microwave on
MEDIUM-HIGH (70%) for an additional 30 seconds. Stir and repeat until completely
melted.

Holding a strawberry by its green cap, dip into the melted white chocolate, covering
completely except for the cap. Place covered strawberry on the waxed paper.
Continue the dipping process until all the melted white chocolate is used. Repeat
process with remaining white chocolate and remaining strawberries. Chill coated
strawberries for 5 to 10 minutes or until set.

In a 1-cup glass measuring cup, or other small and tall microwaveable dish, place half
the semi-sweet chocolate chips. Microwave on MEDIUM-HIGH (70%) for 1 minute;
stir. Microwave on MEDIUM-HIGH (70%) for an additional 30 seconds; stir. Repeat the
process until completely melted.

Holding each strawberry by its cap, dip the strawberry diagonally into the semi-sweet
chocolate to form one side of the tuxedo jacket. Repeat for the other side. Place
dipped strawberry onto waxed paper. Continue the dipping process until all the melted
semi-sweet chocolate is used. Repeat process with most of the remaining semi-sweet
chocolate and remaining strawberries. Chill the strawberries for 5 to 10 minutes or
until set.

Microwave the remaining semi-sweet chocolate on MEDIUM-HIGH (70%) for 30
seconds or until completely melted. Pour the melted chocolate into a small zipper-top
plastic bag. Shake the chocolate into one corner. Press out the air in the bag and seal.
Snip a <u>tiny</u> tip off the corner of the bag to form a pastry decorating bag. Gently
squeeze the chocolate onto the chilled strawberries to form two buttons and a small
bow tie. Chill until ready to serve.

Yield: 24 well-dressed strawberries!

Strawberry Pecan Cookie Stack

Pecan Cookies:
1 cup butter, softened
3/4 cup light brown sugar, packed
1 teaspoon vanilla extract
2 cups flour
1/4 teaspoon cinnamon
1 cup pecans, finely ground

Creamy Filling:
1 cup whipping cream
1/4 cup sugar
1 cup sour cream

Strawberries:
5 cups strawberries, hulled and sliced
1/2 cup sugar

Garnish:
1/3 cup pecans, chopped and toasted

For the Pecan Cookies: Preheat oven to 350° F. Line two jelly roll pans with parchment paper. Lightly spray each pan with cooking spray; set aside.

In a medium bowl, beat the butter until fluffy. Gradually add brown sugar; mix well. Stir in the vanilla extract.

In a small bowl, sift together the flour and cinnamon. Stir in 1 cup pecans. Gradually add to butter mixture and mix well.

Divide dough into 2 equal portions and shape each into a ball. Place one ball in the center of each pan and press into a 10-inch circle.

Bake for 16 to 20 minutes or until golden brown. Cool in pans on wire racks for 10 minutes. Carefully lift cookies on parchment paper from the pans and place on wire racks to cool.

For the Creamy Filling: In a medium bowl, whip the cream and $1/4$ cup sugar until stiff peaks form. Fold in the sour cream. Chill, covered, until ready to use.

For the Strawberries: In a medium bowl, combine the strawberries and $1/2$ cup sugar. Chill, covered, until ready to use.

To assemble: Carefully remove the parchment paper from the cookies. Place one pecan cookie on a large serving plate and spread half the Creamy Filling evenly over the top. Arrange half the strawberries over the Creamy Filling. Place the remaining pecan cookie on top and repeat the layers. Sprinkle with the chopped pecans. Serve immediately.

Yield: 8 to 10 servings

Fresh Strawberry Ambrosia Mousse

2 cups strawberries, hulled and halved
1 cup orange juice, chilled
2 (3-ounce) packages strawberry-
   flavored gelatin
2/3 cup sweetened coconut flakes
1/4 cup sugar
2 cups whipping cream

In a food processor or blender, purée strawberries; drain, reserving the juice. Add water to juice if needed to equal 1/2 cup.

In a medium saucepan, combine orange juice and 1/2 cup reserved juice; bring to a boil over medium-high heat. Remove from heat. Gradually add gelatin, stirring until dissolved. Cool to room temperature.

In a large bowl, combine gelatin mixture, puréed strawberries, coconut and sugar; mix well and set aside.

In a large bowl, beat whipping cream until soft peaks form. Fold whipped cream into the strawberry mixture. Pour into a 2-quart ring mold. Chill, covered, until firm or overnight.

Just before serving, fill kitchen sink with hot water and hold the mold in the water for 1 to 2 minutes or until mousse releases from side of mold. Invert onto a serving platter. Chill, covered, until ready to serve.

Yield: 8 to 10 servings

Showy Meringues with Strawberries & Sorbet

Meringues:
4 egg whites, at room temperature
1/4 teaspoon salt
1/4 teaspoon cream of tartar
I cup sugar
I teaspoon vanilla extract

Strawberries:
3 cups strawberries, hulled and halved
1/3 cup sugar
2 Tablespoons orange-flavored liqueur

Filling:
I pint orange sorbet or sherbet
I cup whipped cream

For the Meringues: Preheat oven to 250° F. Line 2 baking sheets with waxed paper. Spray each lightly with cooking spray; set aside.

In a medium bowl, beat egg whites at medium-low speed until foamy. Add salt and cream of tartar. Increase mixer speed to medium and beat for I minute or until soft peaks form. Gradually add I rounded Tablespoon of the sugar and beat for 30 seconds. Repeat process twice. Add vanilla extract and mix well. Continue to add remaining sugar, I Tablespoon at a time, beating for 30 seconds after each addition until all the sugar is incorporated. Increase mixer speed to high and beat for an additional 7 to 8 minutes.

Spoon meringue onto prepared baking sheets, forming 6 equal mounds. Using a teaspoon, push the center of each meringue outward to form a ring shape with a 2 1/2- to 3-inch hole in the middle.

Bake for I hour. Turn off oven and open the oven door ajar to allow meringues to dry and cool completely. Gently remove from paper. Meringues may be stored in an airtight container.

For the Strawberries: In a medium bowl, combine strawberries, 1/3 cup sugar and liqueur; mix well and set aside.

To assemble: Place each meringue on an individual serving dish. Place one scoop of sorbet in the center of each meringue. Spoon the strawberries over the sorbet. Top each with a dollop of whipped cream. Serve immediately.

Yield: 6 servings

Spiffy Strawberry & Lemon Jelly Roll

Jelly Roll:
4 eggs, separated
3/4 cup sugar, divided
1/2 teaspoon vanilla extract
3/4 cup flour
1 teaspoon baking powder
1/2 teaspoon salt
1/3 cup powdered sugar

Strawberry Butter Cream Frosting:
1 cup butter, softened
3 Tablespoons strawberry preserves
1 teaspoon vanilla extract
2 cups powdered sugar, sifted

Strawberry Lemon Filling:
2 (8-ounce) containers lemon yogurt
1/2 cup powdered sugar, sifted
2 cups strawberries, hulled and sliced

Garnish:
3 strawberries, whole with caps

For the Jelly Roll: Preheat oven to 375° F. Lightly spray a 10 x 15-inch jelly roll pan with cooking spray. Line the bottom of the pan with a piece of waxed paper. Lightly spray the waxed paper with cooking spray; set aside.

In a small bowl, beat 4 egg yolks until smooth. Gradually beat in 1/4 cup sugar and vanilla extract. Wash mixer blades thoroughly.

In a medium bowl, beat 4 egg whites until soft peaks form. Gradually beat in 1/2 cup sugar and beat until stiff peaks form. Fold the egg yolks into the egg whites.

Sift together the flour, baking powder and salt. Fold the flour mixture into the egg mixture. Spread the batter evenly over the bottom of the prepared pan.

Bake for 12 minutes or until golden brown.

Lay a clean dishtowel out flat and sprinkle evenly with 1/3 cup powdered sugar.

Remove the cake from the oven. Immediately loosen the sides of the cake with a knife and turn out onto prepared towel. Remove waxed paper. Quickly place a fresh sheet of waxed paper on top of cake and roll the cake tightly with the paper on the inside. Wrap cake in sugared towel. Place on a wire rack and cool completely.

For the Strawbery Butter Cream Frosting: In a medium bowl, beat butter until light and fluffy. Add strawberry preserves and vanilla extract; mix well. Gradually add powdered sugar and mix well. Chill, covered, until ready to use.

To assemble: Unroll cake and remove waxed paper. Spread the yogurt evenly over the top of the cake. Arrange strawberry slices over yogurt, creating Strawberry Lemon Filling. Re-roll and place seam side down on a serving platter.

Spread frosting evenly over the jelly roll. Garnish with whole strawberries. Chill, covered, for 3 hours.

Yield: 10 to 12 servings

Heavenly Strawberry Bavarian

1 cup strawberries, hulled and
    sliced
1/4 cup sugar
1 (3-ounce) package
    strawberry-flavored gelatin
1 cup boiling water
3/4 cup orange juice, chilled
1 prepared angel food cake
2 1/2 cups whipping cream,
    divided
3 Tablespoons powdered sugar
1/2 teaspoon vanilla extract
6 strawberries, whole
    with caps

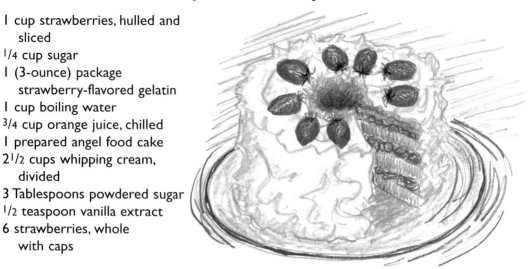

In a medium bowl, combine the sliced strawberries and sugar; mix well. Chill, covered, until ready to use.

In a small bowl, combine the gelatin and boiling water; stir until completely dissolved. Stir in the orange juice. Chill, covered, until the gelatin is slightly thickened.

Cut the angel food cake into 1-inch cubes and place in a medium bowl; set aside.

In a large bowl, beat 1 cup of the whipping cream until stiff peaks form. Fold the whipped cream into the gelatin mixture. Drain the strawberries and stir into the gelatin mixture.

Lightly spray a 10-inch tube pan with cooking spray. Alternate layers of cake cubes and strawberry mixture, pressing lightly after each layer. Chill, covered, overnight.

Unmold the dessert onto a serving plate.

In a medium bowl, beat the remaining 1 1/2 cups whipping cream with powdered sugar and vanilla extract until stiff peaks form. Spread the whipped cream over the side and top of the dessert. Chill, covered, until ready to serve.

Garnish with whole strawberries.

Yield: 10 to 12 servings

Stunning Strawberries with Orange Liqueur

6 cups strawberries, hulled and halved
3/4 cup pecans, chopped
1/3 cup sugar
1/4 cup Grand Marnier
2 teaspoons orange zest
1/4 teaspoon cinnamon
2 cups whipped cream
6 strawberries, whole with caps
6 pecan halves

In a medium bowl, combine strawberry halves, 3/4 cup chopped pecans, sugar, Grand Marnier, orange zest and cinnamon; toss gently. Marinate for 15 minutes at room temperature or chill, covered, until ready to use.

Just before serving, spoon strawberries equally into six glass dishes or large wine glasses. Add 1/3 cup dollop of whipped cream to the top or to the side of each serving. Place a whole strawberry and pecan half in the center of the whipped cream. Serve immediately.

Yield: 6 servings

Superb Strawberry Almond Tart

Tart Shell:
3/4 cup flour
1/2 cup almonds, finely ground
2 Tablespoons powdered sugar
1/2 cup butter, chilled and cut into pieces

Almond Filling:
1/3 cup sugar
1/4 cup almonds, finely ground
3/4 cup whipping cream
1 egg, beaten
1 teaspoon vanilla extract
1/4 teaspoon almond extract
1/4 teaspoon salt

Strawberry Crown:
1/2 cup apricot preserves
1 Tablespoon almond liqueur
1 quart strawberries, hulled and halved
1 cup whipped cream or whipped
   topping, thawed
1 strawberry, whole with cap

For the Tart Shell: Preheat oven to 425° F.

In a food processor, combine the flour, 1/2 cup almonds and powdered sugar; mix well. Add the butter and process until the mixture resembles coarse meal. Quickly press the mixture firmly into an 11-inch fluted tart pan with a removable bottom.

Bake for 8 to 10 minutes. Cool on a wire rack and loosen slightly.

For the Almond Filling: Preheat oven to 375° F.

In a medium bowl, combine the sugar and 1/4 cup almonds; mix well. Add the whipping cream, egg, vanilla extract, almond extract and salt; mix well. Pour mixture into the cooled tart shell.

Bake for 40 to 45 minutes or until browned. Cool the tart in pan on a wire rack for 1 hour.

For the Strawberry Crown: In a small saucepan, combine the apricot preserves and almond liqueur; mix well. Cook over medium heat until blended, stirring constantly and removing any large pieces of apricot.

Arrange the strawberry halves on top of the tart with cut sides down. Spoon the apricot mixture over the strawberries.

Remove the tart from the pan. Spoon dollops of whipped cream around the edge and place one dollop in the center. Top the center dollop with whole strawberry.

Yield: 8 servings

Sassy Strawberry Tacos

Cookie Taco Shells:
6 Tablespoons unsalted butter, softened
3/4 cup sugar
3 egg whites, slightly beaten
1/2 teaspoon vanilla extract
Pinch of salt
3/4 cup flour

Filling:
2 cups bananas, sliced
2 teaspoons lemon juice
4 1/2 cups strawberries, hulled and
   halved, divided
3 Tablespoons sugar
1 1/2 cups kiwi, peeled and sliced 1/4-inch-
   thick
1 cup sweetened coconut flakes
6 to 8 drops yellow food coloring
1 cup whipped cream

For the Cookie Taco Shells: Preheat oven to 350° F. Line 2 baking sheets with parchment paper. Using a pencil, draw two 6 1/2-inch circles onto each sheet; set aside.

Place 2 tall drinking glasses upside down and at least 7 inches apart on a counter. Suspend two wooded spoons on top of the glasses with the handles next to each other to form a bar. Repeat with another 2 glasses and 2 wooden spoons.

In a medium mixing bowl with an electric mixer, cream together the butter and sugar until light and fluffy. Beat in the egg whites, vanilla extract and salt until blended. Gently fold in the flour.

Anchor the parchment paper to the baking sheets by placing a small dab of batter under each corner. Using a rubber spatula, spread a thin layer of the batter inside each circle on the parchment paper.

Bake for 6 to 8 minutes, or until golden and browned on the edges. Remove the cookies from the oven. Quickly but carefully slide a metal spatula under a cookie. Lift and drape the cookie evenly over the wooden spoon bar to form the taco shell. Repeat with the remaining cookie. When cooled, gently remove the cookies and place on a plate; repeat the process with remaining batter.

Cookie shells may be prepared 3 days ahead; store in an airtight container at room temperature.

For the Filling: In a small bowl, mash the bananas. Stir in the lemon juice. Chill, covered, until ready to use.

In a blender or food processor, combine 1 1/2 cups strawberries with the sugar; purée until smooth. Pour into a small mixing bowl and chill, covered, until ready to use.

In a small bowl, toss the coconut with yellow food coloring until combined; set aside.

Cut kiwi slices in half to form crescents.

To assemble: Place each shell on an individual serving plate. Spoon 1/4 cup mashed bananas into each shell. Top each with 1/2 cup sliced strawberries and 1/4 cup kiwi. Drizzle 1 1/2 Tablespoons strawberry purée over fruit. Sprinkle with coconut. Top with a dollop of whipped cream. Serve immediately.

Yield: 6 tacos

White & Dark Chocolate Strawberry Pie

1 (9-inch) pie shell, baked

Dark Chocolate Layer:
1/2 cup hot fudge sauce, at room
    temperature
1/2 cup macadamia nuts, salted and
    chopped

White Chocolate Layer:
1 cup white chocolate chips
1 (8-ounce) package cream cheese,
    softened
1 teaspoon vanilla extract
1 (8-ounce) container frozen whipped
    topping, thawed

Strawberry Layer:
1/3 cup orange marmalade
2 teaspoons sugar
4 cups strawberries, hulled and halved

Garnish:
3 Tablespoons semi-sweet chocolate
    chips
3 Tablespoons white chocolate chips

For the Dark Chocolate Layer: Spread hot fudge sauce evenly over the bottom of the pie shell. Sprinkle macadamia nuts evenly over the top and gently press nuts into hot fudge sauce; set aside.

For the White Chocolate Layer: In a small microwaveable dish, heat white chocolate chips on MEDIUM-HIGH (70%) for 60 seconds. Stir until smooth. Set aside to cool slightly.

In a medium bowl, beat cream cheese until smooth. Beat in melted chocolate and vanilla extract; mix well. Fold in whipped topping and mix completely.

Spread mixture evenly into the prepared pie shell; set aside.

For the Strawberry Layer: In a small saucepan, combine orange marmalade and sugar; mix well. Place the pan over medium heat and boil for 1 minute, stirring constantly. Remove from heat; set aside.

Arrange strawberries on top of pie with cut sides down. Spoon the marmalade mixture evenly over the strawberries.

For the Garnish: In a small microwaveable dish, heat semi-sweet chocolate chips on MEDIUM-HIGH (70%) for 45 seconds. Stir until smooth. Pour melted chocolate into a small zipper-top plastic bag. Shake chocolate into one corner. Press out the air in the bag and seal. Snip a <u>tiny</u> tip off the corner of the bag to form a pastry decorating bag. Drizzle melted chocolate randomly over the top of the pie. Repeat process with white chocolate chips.

Chill, covered, for 2 hours before serving.

Yield: 8 to 10 servings

Splendid Strawberry Drop Cobbler

Strawberry Filling:
5 cups strawberries, hulled and halved
1/2 cup light brown sugar,
   packed
3 Tablespoons orange juice
1/2 teaspoon cinnamon

Golden Drop Biscuits:
1 cup flour
3 Tablespoons sugar
1 teaspoon baking powder
1/2 teaspoon baking soda
1/4 teaspoon salt
2 Tablespoons butter,
   chilled and cut into pieces
1/2 cup sour cream

Topping:
2 Tablespoons sugar
1/2 teaspoon cinnamon

For the Strawberry Filling: Lightly spray a 9-inch square baking dish with cooking spray; set aside.

In a medium saucepan, combine strawberries, brown sugar, orange juice and cinnamon; mix well. Place pan over medium-high heat and bring to a boil. Reduce the heat and simmer, uncovered, for 5 minutes, stirring occasionally. Pour the mixture into the prepared baking dish.

For the Golden Drop Biscuits: Preheat oven to 350° F.

In a medium bowl, combine flour, 3 Tablespoons sugar, baking powder, baking soda and salt; mix well. Using a pastry blender, cut the butter into mixture until it forms coarse crumbs. Add the sour cream and stir until mixture forms a ball of dough. Shape the dough into 1-inch balls and place them on top of the strawberry mixture.

For the Topping: In a small bowl, combine the 2 Tablespoons sugar and cinnamon; mix well. Sprinkle over the top of the biscuits.

Bake, covered with aluminum foil, for 15 minutes. Remove the foil and bake for an additional 10 minutes. Let cool slightly on a wire rack and serve while warm.

Yield: 4 to 6 servings

Strawberry White Chocolate Tiramisu

1 (12-ounce) package white chocolate
   chips
2 Tablespoons milk
2 (8-ounce) packages cream cheese,
   softened
1 (8-ounce) container frozen whipped
   topping, thawed
36 to 42 ladyfingers, crispy-style
3/4 cup strong black coffee
1/4 cup plus 1 teaspoon coffee-flavored
   liqueur, divided
1 cup strawberries, hulled and sliced
1 1/2 cups strawberries, hulled and
   halved
1/4 cup light corn syrup

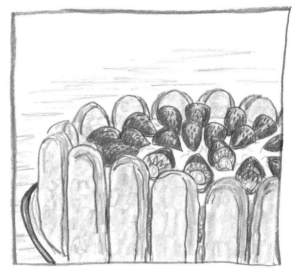

In a small microwaveable dish, heat white chocolate chips on MEDIUM-HIGH (70%) for 60 seconds; stir. Microwave on MEDIUM-HIGH (70%) for an additional 30 seconds; stir until melted. Gradually stir in milk, 1 teaspoon at a time. Set aside to cool.

In a large mixing bowl, beat cream cheese for 30 seconds. Gradually pour in white chocolate mixture, beating constantly. Fold in whipped topping; set aside.

In a 9-inch springform pan, stand ladyfingers up around edge of pan with the flat side facing in. You can cut the ends off the cookies if they are too tall for the pan. Arrange half the remaining ladyfingers over the bottom of the pan. You can use the extra end pieces to fill in any gaps.

In a small bowl, combine coffee and 1/4 cup coffee liqueur; mix well. Brush or sprinkle half the coffee mixture over the ladyfingers in the bottom of the pan.

Spoon half the white chocolate mixture evenly over the ladyfingers. Arrange sliced strawberries over the white chocolate layer. Layer the remaining ladyfingers, coffee mixture and white chocolate mixture over the top. Arrange remaining strawberry halves, cut side down, evenly over the top of the white chocolate layer.

In a small bowl, combine corn syrup and 1 teaspoon coffee liqueur; mix well. Brush or spoon over strawberry halves. Chill, covered, for 4 hours or overnight.

Remove springform ring and place tiramisu on a cake stand or serving plate. Chill, covered, until ready to serve.

Yield: 10 to 12 servings

Strawberry Supreme Cheesecake

Crust:
1/2 cup walnuts, ground
1 cup graham cracker crumbs
3 Tablespoons butter, melted

Filling:
4 (8-ounce) packages cream cheese,
    softened
5 eggs, at room temperature, beaten
1/2 cup sugar
1 Tablespoon lemon juice
2 teaspoons vanilla extract
1/2 teaspoon almond extract

Creamy Layer:
2 cups sour cream
1/3 cup sugar
1 teaspoon vanilla extract

Strawberry Crown:
1/2 cup red currant jelly
1 Tablespoon sugar
4 cups strawberries, hulled and halved

For the Crust: Preheat oven to 350° F. Lightly spray a 10-inch springform pan with cooking spray; set aside.

In a medium bowl, combine walnuts, graham cracker crumbs and melted butter; mix well. Press mixture firmly and evenly over the bottom of the pan.

For the Filling: In a large bowl, beat cream cheese until smooth. Add eggs, 1/2 cup sugar, lemon juice, vanilla extract and almond extract; mix well. Spoon the mixture into prepared pan.

Place the pan on a baking sheet. Bake for 40 to 45 minutes. Don't worry if the cheesecake cracks; it will settle as it cools and topping will cover the cracks.

Remove and place cheesecake pan on a wire rack to cool for 15 minutes. Leave the oven on 350° F.

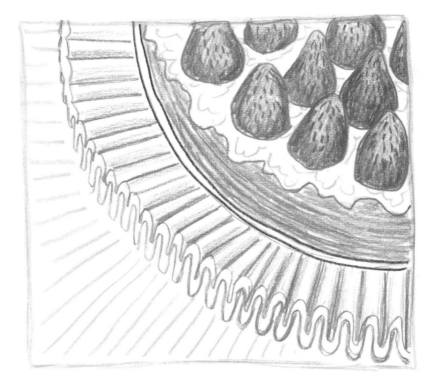

For the Creamy Layer: In a medium bowl, combine sour cream, sugar and vanilla extract; mix well. Spoon the mixture onto the center of the cheesecake and spread evenly over the center, extending outward to ¹/2 inch from the edge. Bake at 350° F for 5 minutes. Remove from oven and cool in the pan, on a wire rack for 1 hour. Chill, covered, overnight or up to 2 days.

For the Strawberry Crown: In a small saucepan, combine jelly and sugar. Place the pan over medium heat and boil for 1 minute, stirring constantly. Remove from heat; set aside.

Using a knife, loosen the cheesecake from the side of the pan and remove the springform ring.

Arrange strawberries, cut side down, on the top of the cheesecake. Spoon the jelly mixture evenly over strawberries, allowing the glaze to drip down the sides of the cheesecake. Chill, covered, until glaze is set.

Yield: 10 to 12 servings

Scrumptious Strawberry Charlotte

2 envelopes unflavored gelatin
$^1/4$ cup water
1 (8-ounce) package cream cheese, softened
1 (3.4-ounce) package vanilla instant
   pudding
1 cup butter, melted
1 cup sugar
$^1/3$ cup plain yogurt
2 cups whipping cream, divided
36 ladyfingers, crispy-style
1 to 2 Tablespoons Grand Marnier
1 quart strawberries, hulled and sliced
$^1/3$ cup powdered sugar
$^1/2$ teaspoon vanilla extract

In a small saucepan, sprinkle gelatin into the water and let stand for 1 minute. Place over medium heat and stir until gelatin is dissolved. Remove from heat and set aside.

In a medium bowl, beat cream cheese until smooth. Add the pudding mix, melted butter, sugar and yogurt; mix until smooth. Gradually stir in gelatin mixture and mix well.

In medium bowl, whip 1 cup whipping cream until stiff peaks form. Fold into cream cheese mixture; set aside.

Place a circle of waxed paper in the bottom of a 9-inch springform pan. Stand ladyfingers up around edge of pan with the flat side facing in. You can cut the ends off the cookies if they are too tall for the pan. Arrange the remaining ladyfingers over the bottom of the pan. You can use the extra end pieces to fill in any gaps.

Brush or sprinkle Grand Marnier lightly over the ladyfingers. Be careful not to overmoisten as ladyfingers will disintegrate.

Spoon half the cream cheese mixture into the pan. Arrange half the strawberries over the cream cheese layer. Spoon remaining cream cheese mixture over strawberry layer. Chill, covered, for 8 to 12 hours or until firm. Also chill remaining strawberries in a covered container.

Before serving, beat remaining 1 cup whipping cream with powdered sugar and vanilla extract until stiff peaks form. Spread whipped cream over top of charlotte. Arrange strawberries decoratively on top of whipped cream. Remove springform ring. Place charlotte on a cake stand or serving plate. Chill, covered, until ready to serve.

Yield: 10 to 12 servings

Snazzy Strawberry Chocolate Trifle

1 cup semi-sweet chocolate chips
3 (8-ounce) containers vanilla yogurt
1/2 cup sugar
3 Tablespoons almond liqueur or
   1/2 teaspoon almond extract
12 to 16 ladyfingers, crispy-style
4 cups strawberries, hulled and halved
1 cup whipped cream
1/3 cup almond slivers, toasted
6 strawberries, whole with caps

In a small microwaveable bowl, heat chocolate chips on MEDIUM-HIGH (70%) for 30 seconds; stir. Heat for an additional 30 seconds on MEDIUM-HIGH (70%); stir. Repeat process until chips are completely melted and smooth. Let cool slightly.

In a medium bowl, combine yogurt, sugar and almond liqueur; mix well. Add melted chocolate and mix well.

In a trifle bowl or a tall clear glass bowl, 8 inches in diameter, layer half the ladyfingers, half the strawberries and half the chocolate mixture at a time; repeat layers. Chill, covered, at least 2 hours.

Just before serving, top with whipped cream. Sprinkle toasted almonds over whipped cream. Garnish with whole strawberries.

Yield: 8 to 10 servings

Simple Strawberry Shortcakes

Shortcakes:
1³/4 cups flour
1 Tablespoon baking powder
1 Tablespoon sugar
¹/2 teaspoon salt
¹/4 cup butter, chilled and cut into pieces
²/3 cup milk
1 egg, beaten
¹/2 teaspoon water

Strawberries:
6 cups strawberries, hulled and halved
¹/2 cup sugar
¹/2 teaspoon lemon juice

Whipped Cream:
2 cups whipping cream
¹/4 cup powdered sugar
¹/2 teaspoon vanilla extract

For the Shortcakes: Preheat oven to 425° F. Lightly spray a large baking sheet with cooking spray.

In a medium bowl, sift together the flour, baking powder, sugar and salt. Using a pastry blender, cut in the butter until mixture is crumbly. Gradually add the milk and stir just until moistened. Do not over blend.

On a floured cutting board, gently pat out the dough to about ¹/2-inch thickness. Using a 3-inch biscuit cutter, or similar-size decorative cookie cutter, cut out shortcakes and place on prepared pan.

In a small bowl, combine the egg and water; mix well. Brush the egg mixture over the tops of the shortcakes.

Bake for 15 minutes or until golden brown. Remove to a wire rack to cool completely.

For the Strawberries: In a medium bowl, combine strawberries, sugar and lemon juice; mix well. Chill, covered, until ready to use.

For the Whipped Cream: In a large bowl, combine whipping cream, powdered sugar and vanilla extract; beat until stiff peaks form. Chill, covered, until ready to use.

To assemble: Split each shortcake in half horizontally. Place each bottom half on an individual serving dish. Top each with strawberries and a dollop of whipped cream. Place remaining shortcake half on top and spoon on more strawberries and whipped cream. Serve immediately.

You may cut the shortcakes into heart shapes for an extra-special presentation.

Yield: 8 to 10 servings

Unbelievable Chocolate Strawberry Shortcakes

Shortcakes:
1 cup flour
1/2 cup sugar
1/4 cup unsweetened cocoa powder
1 1/2 Tablespoons baking powder
1 teaspoon baking soda
1/4 teaspoon nutmeg
1/4 teaspoon salt
5 Tablespoons butter, melted
1/3 cup milk
2/3 cup sweetened coconut flakes
2/3 cup pecans, chopped

Strawberries:
5 cups strawberries, hulled and halved
1/2 cup sugar

Whipped Cream:
1 1/2 cups whipping cream
1/2 cup powdered sugar
1/2 teaspoon vanilla extract

Garnish:
6 Tablespoons chocolate sauce
6 strawberries, whole with caps

For the Shortcakes: Preheat oven to 425° F.

In a medium bowl, combine flour, 1/2 cup sugar, cocoa, baking powder, baking soda, nutmeg and salt; mix well. Add the melted butter, milk, coconut and pecans; stir just until combined. Shape by Tablespoonfuls into six 2 1/4-inch balls. Place 2 inches apart on 2 baking sheets.

Bake for 12 to 15 minutes or just until a wooden pick inserted in the centers comes out clean. Remove pans to a wire rack and cool completely.

For the Strawberries: In a medium bowl, combine halved strawberries and sugar; toss to coat. Chill, covered, until ready to use.

For the Whipped Cream: In a medium bowl, whip cream, powdered sugar and vanilla extract until stiff peaks form. Chill, covered, until ready to use.

To assemble: Slice a cooled shortcake in half horizontally. Place the bottom half on an individual serving dish. Spread a dollop of whipped cream over the top. Spoon on strawberries. Place shortcake top on strawberry layer and add more whipped cream and strawberries. Drizzle with 1 Tablespoon of the chocolate sauce. Garnish with a whole strawberry. Repeat process with the remaining ingredients and serve.

Yield: 6 servings

Surprising Strawberry Gifts

Snappy Strawberry Orange Jam

2 cups puréed strawberries
4 cups sugar
1/2 teaspoon cinnamon
1 Tablespoon Grand Marnier
2 teaspoons orange zest
1 (1.75-ounce) package powdered
   fruit pectin
1 cup water
6 1/2 pint canning jars, lids and seals

In a medium bowl, combine strawberries,
sugar, cinnamon, Grand Marnier and
orange zest; mix well. Let stand for 20 minutes.

In a medium saucepan, combine pectin and water; mix well. Over medium-high heat,
boil for 1 minute, stirring constantly. Remove from heat and stir in strawberries;
continue stirring for 3 minutes.

Pour equal amounts of the hot mixture into six 1/2-pint canning jars. Seal and screw
lids on tightly. Let stand at room temperature for 1 hour. Keep chilled until ready to
use.

Yield: six 1/2-pint jars

Spicy & Sweet Strawberry Bar-b-que Sauce

2 cups strawberries, hulled and sliced
1/3 cup strawberry preserves
1/2 cup catsup
2 Tablespoons honey
3 Tablespoons soy sauce
2 Tablespoons lemon juice
2 Tablespoons ground ginger
1/2 teaspoon red pepper sauce
1/4 teaspoon salt
3 Tablespoons green onions, chopped

Combine all ingredients in a food
processor and purée until smooth. Pour the sauce into a jar and chill, covered, until
ready to use.

Yield: 2 cups

Delightful Strawberry Chutney

3/4 cup golden raisins
2/3 cup light brown sugar, packed
1/2 cup strawberry preserves
1/2 cup red wine vinegar
1/2 cup orange juice
1 envelope unflavored gelatin
1 teaspoon ground ginger
1/2 teaspoon curry powder
6 drops red pepper sauce
1 (11-ounce) can mandarin oranges,
   drained and coarsely chopped
4 cups strawberries, hulled and chopped
3/4 cup sliced almonds
5 1/2-pint canning jars, lids and seals

In a large, non-aluminum saucepan, combine raisins, brown sugar, preserves, vinegar, orange juice, gelatin, ginger, curry powder, red pepper sauce and oranges; bring to a boil. Cook, uncovered, over medium heat for 15 minutes or until slightly thickened, stirring frequently. Add strawberries and reduce heat. Simmer, uncovered, for 10 minutes or until thickened, stirring frequently. Remove from heat and stir in almonds.

Spoon equal amounts into five 1/2-pint canning jars. Seal and screw lids on tightly. Let stand at room temperature for 1 hour. Chill until ready to use.

Yield: 5 cups

Smooth Strawberry Cream Cheese

1 (8-ounce) package cream cheese,
   softened
1/4 cup powdered sugar
1 teaspoon orange zest
3/4 cup strawberries, hulled and sliced

In a small bowl, blend the cream cheese, powdered sugar and orange zest until smooth. Add the strawberries and mix until blended. Spoon into a covered container. Chill, covered, until ready to use.

Yield: 1 1/4 cups

Strawberry Apple Cider Vinegar

4 cups strawberries, hulled and halved
4 cups apple cider vinegar
1/4 cup sugar
18 strawberries, whole and hulled
6 1/2-pint canning jars, lids and seals

In a blender, purée 4 cups strawberries.
In a medium glass bowl, combine
strawberry purée, vinegar and sugar; mix
until sugar is dissolved. Chill, covered,
for 2 days.

Place a fine sieve over a medium bowl.
Pour the strawberry mixture into the sieve to strain. Do NOT squeeze the remaining
pulp. Discard the seeds and pulp.

Pour juice into a medium saucepan. Bring to a boil over medium-high heat and boil for
1 minute. Remove the pan from heat.

Place 3 whole strawberries in each of six 1/2-pint canning jars. Pour equal amounts of
the hot juice into the jars, leaving 1/2-inch space at top of each jar. Seal and screw lids
on tightly. Store in a cool dark place for three weeks before using.

Yield: 3 cups

Strawberry Orange Butter Spread

1 pint strawberries, hulled and sliced
1 cup unsalted butter, softened
1 cup powdered sugar, sifted
1 teaspoon orange zest
1 teaspoon Grand Marnier or orange
 juice

Place all ingredients in a food processor or blender and blend until smooth and creamy.
Spoon the mixture into a serving dish. Chill, covered, until ready to use. The mixture
will keep in the refrigerator for two weeks.

Yield: approximately 2 cups

Index

Index

Order information

To order additional copies of *Simple Strawberry Sensations!*,
include Your Name, Complete Address, Telephone Number *(including area code)*
and quantity of cookbooks to:

Simple Sensations Marketing, LLC
533 S. Howard Avenue #855
Tampa, Florida 33606
813-832-4482
813-835-4205 (fax)

Per copy	$12.95
Postage and handling	3.95
Total	$16.90

(Note: Florida residents add $.91 sales tax for a total of $17.81)

Make checks payable to: Simple Sensations Marketing, LLC
Allow three weeks delivery.